ALONG THE
ROUTE
of the ACE

LAURIE GOLDEN

Ian Allan
PUBLISHING

FRONT COVER Rebuilt 'Merchant Navy' class 4-6-2 No 35026 *Lamport & Holt Line* is seen leaving Salisbury for Waterloo on the up 'Atlantic Coast Express' with its usual load of 11 coaches on Saturday 4th May 1963. The Exmouth Junction crew had converted a two minute late departure from Exeter Central into a two minute early arrival at Salisbury. This was the last year the headboard was used regularly but it can still be seen gracing the front of the sectioned 'Merchant Navy' class No 35029 in the National Railway Museum at York. *Mark B. Warburton*

TITLE PAGE 'Battle of Britain' class 4-6-2 No 34081 *92 Squadron* is seen heading east through the cutting between Meldon Junction and Meldon viaduct on Tuesday 30th July 1963. The train started from Padstow at 09.33. The down home signal for Meldon Junction can be seen to the left of the train and to the right the out-of-use up refuge siding. After withdrawal in 1964, No 34081 was rescued from Woodham's yard at Barry in 1973 by the Battle of Britain Locomotive Society, and is currently being overhauled at Wansford on the Nene Valley Railway.

BACK COVER 'Merchant Navy' class 4-6-2 No 35026 *Lamport & Holt* restarts the 'ACE' from a signal check at Honiton (see page 65 for further information).

First published 2015

ISBN 978 0 7110 3698 7

Published by Ian Allan Publishing Ltd, Hersham, Surrey, KT12 4RG

Printed in China

Visit the Ian Allan Publishing website at *www.ianallanpublishing.com*

All the photographs were taken by the author unless otherwise credited.

Introduction

The Atlantic Coast Express (ACE) made its inaugural run from Waterloo at 11.00am on 19 July 1926. It had five destinations – Plymouth, Torrington and Ilfracombe in Devon, and Padstow and Bude in Cornwall. In later years, portions for Sidmouth and Exmouth were detached at Sidmouth Junction. Services continued in much the same pattern until the outbreak of World War 2. After the war, the ACE was soon re-introduced, still with the 11.00am departure from Waterloo. By this time, 'Merchant Navy' Pacifics were available to work from Waterloo to Exeter Central. From there, weight restrictions necessitated the use of 'West Country' and 'Battle of Britain' Light Pacifics.

Between Salisbury and Exeter, the route makes a gradual climb westwards towards Semley, thence undulating progress to Yeovil with a number of short but significant gradients of about 1 in 100. Now heading in a more southwesterly direction, the route makes a significant summit at Crewkerne before descending into Axminster and Seaton Junction. Here started the most significant bank on the route, the six-mile climb at mainly 1 in 80 to a summit at the western end of Honiton Tunnel. After a descent at mainly 1 in 100 to Sidmouth Junction, the route undulates with generally less severe gradients into Exeter Central station.

After a sharp descent from Exeter Central to the GWR station at St Davids, the SR services headed north on GWR metals for about a mile, before diverging northwestwards on its own line at Cowley Bridge Junction. The line followed the Yeo Valley past Crediton to Colebrooke Junction, at which point the Ilfracombe route headed north and the Padstow/Bude/Plymouth trains diverged west. The northbound route continued to follow easy gradients through to Barnstaple, where the Torrington branch diverged south-westwards close to the shores of the River Taw. Having crossed the Taw, Ilfracombe-bound trains faced a severe climb from Braunton to Mortehoe, followed by an equally severe descent into the terminus at Ilfracombe. On summer Saturdays, variety of traffic was enhanced by GWR trains from the line from Taunton, which joined the SR route at Barnstaple, being extended to Ilfracombe still with their GWR locomotive.

Having diverged from the Ilfracombe line at Coleford Junction, the 'North Cornwall' line climbed around the north-eastern edge of Dartmoor to Okehampton, approximately 1,000ft above sea level. The climb continued another couple of miles to Meldon where it crossed the River Okement on a 120ft high wrought iron truss girder viaduct.

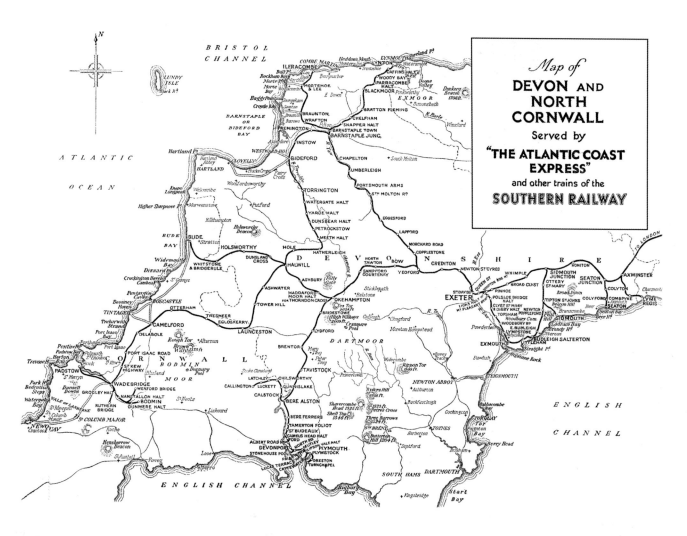

The weight limit on this structure restricted the types of locomotives, which could be used on this route. Shortly afterwards, the Plymouth line diverged south westwards to skirt Yes Tor, the highest point on Dartmoor, and follow the western edge of the Moor through Tavistock towards its ultimate destination. Meanwhile, the North Cornwall line took a meandering descent in a generally north-westward direction to Halwill, the junction for Bude and Padstow. The descent continued westwards to the coast at Bude, whereas the Padstow line headed south westwards around the northwestern edge of Bodmin Moor, with a number of significant gradients though Launceston and Camelford to eventually reach Wadebridge and Padstow.

On summer Saturdays, during the late 1950s and early 1960s, the large amount of holiday traffic required the train to be run in several portions. Departing from London's Waterloo station, all trains stopped at Salisbury (for water) and Exeter Central and St Davids. By 1963, the ACE divided at Exeter Central, with separate portions leaving within 10 minutes of each other for Ilfracombe/Torrington, and Padstow/Bude with a connection at Okehampton for Plymouth. In the summer months, the two portions ran as separate trains from Waterloo, the Padstow/Bude departing five minutes later at 11.05.

In its last year of 1964, there was a 10.15 departure calling additionally at Templecombe, Seaton Junction and Barnstaple Junction, then all stations to Ilfracombe. Next was the 10.35 departure calling additionally only at Axminster and Halwill Junction, then virtually all stations to Padstow and Bude. Then came the traditional 11.00 departure calling additionally at Sidmouth Junction,

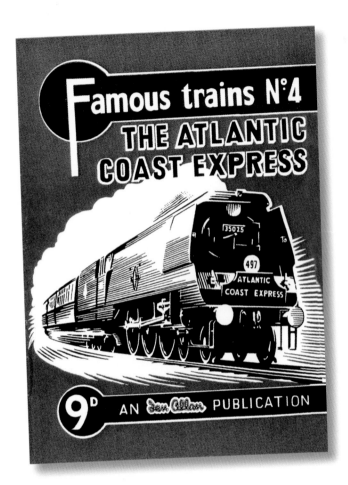

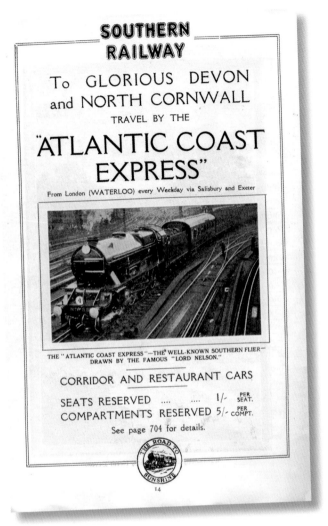

Eggesford and Barnstaple Junction, then all stations to Ilfracombe. Finally, there was an 11.15 departure, calling additionally at Yeovil Junction, North Tawton, and Okehampton, then all stations (including Maddaford Moor Halt!) to Padstow, with a connection to Bude. There were, of course, corresponding 'up' workings from all these destinations.

The last run of the ACE was on 5 September 1964, thereafter the motive power depot at Exmouth Junction closed and all remaining services west of Exeter became diesel-operated. The decline continued, with Torrington losing its passenger service in 1965, the North Cornwall (Padstow and Bude) branches in 1966, Okehampton to Plymouth in 1968 and Barnstaple to Ilfracombe in 1970.

Being born and brought up in Surbiton, it is perhaps no surprise that my principal railway interest was in the Southern Region (SR) of the then British Railways (BR). When the Southern lines west of Salisbury were put under Western Region (WR) control from January 1963, I realised that the 'writing was on the wall' for steam services,

particularly those lines west of Exeter, the so-called 'Withered Arm'. I had previously made short trips to the area, photographing in black and white some of the final workings with ex-LSWR 'T9' 4-4-0s, but having just started colour photography, I decided to make a tour of these lines by train during the more intensive summer service of 1963. I had had for a number of years a lineside pass covering all the non-electrified lines of the SR, and early in 1963 I was able to obtain from Paddington a lineside pass for all the ex-SR lines west of Salisbury.

I planned a trip with my friend, the late Bill Sumner, to commence on Friday 26 July, travelling down to Exeter on the 01.15 newspaper train from Waterloo, which arrived at Exeter around 05.00. Having spent Friday photographing the Exe Valley branch of the former GWR, I travelled on Saturday morning to Mortehoe on the Taunton-

Barnstaple line, the GWR services being extended to Ilfracombe on summer Saturdays. From then onwards, my time was spentphotographing on the route of the ACE.

Mortehoe, on the SR line from Exeter to Ilfracombe, was of considerable interest to me as it was the summit of severe climbs from both the north and south. The remainder of the day was spent photographing either side of Mortehoe, followed on Sunday going south of Barnstaple with the rather sparse service. Moving around by train, it was often expedient to photograph the train on which I travelled either arriving or departing a station, also on occasions jumping out and taking a photograph before boarding again to continue the journey on the same train. This was certainly necessary on Monday, as we were taking the morning train from Torrington to Halwill Junction. With only one morning and one evening train per day in each direction, there was no way we would waste time waiting around for the best part of the day with little to photograph at any specific location.

The remainder of this and the next day was spent on the line towards Wadebridge, then back towards Okehampton and Yeoford. The final day of this trip was spent on the southern part of the line from Yeoford to Barnstaple, as far north as Lapford. One remarkable feature was that throughout the whole five days, we had cloudless sunny days! As will be seen from the photographs, little had changed operationally in the seven months of WR operation, with the expected SR motive power of the period, 'N' class 2-6-0s and 'West Country' and Battle of Britain' class 4-6-2s, still primarily in evidence. However, from June 1963, trains on the Okehampton to Plymouth line became diesel-hauled, with the exception of the through Brighton–Plymouth and the occasional freight.

I made a further visit to the area in July 1964 with another colleague, Peter Brown, this time by car. By now, the 'old order' was definitely in decline. The Barnstaple line had become diesel-operated, and, although the Padstow and Bude lines were still steam-hauled, BR Class 4MT 2-6-4Ts had been drafted in to replace many of the 'N' class and some of the Pacific workings. In fact, the major part of the trip was to cover the ex-SR main line from Exeter to Salisbury, the subject of the second section of this book.

Here, the Bulleid Pacifics still ruled the way, along again with the occasional 'N' and also BR Class 5MT 4-6-0s, which were quite capable of maintaining all but the fastest express schedules. This line was the stamping ground of the 'Merchant Navies', by then all rebuilt, which had always been banned west of Exeter Central. West of Exeter, original 'Light Pacifics' prevailed – rebuilt ones were certainly banned from the Ilfracombe line because of their increased weight, and only once did I see a rebuilt Pacific working on the Okehampton route.

The 110 'Light Pacifics' were nominally classified as 'West Country' and 'Battle of Britain' in roughly equal numbers, the difference between them being merely in the names they were given. When built, most of the 'Battle of Britain' class was allocated to the Kent lines, their names commemorating aircraft, airfields, squadrons and personalities connected with the famous aerial battle of 1940. The 'West Countrys' were allocated over the rest of the SR, including Exmouth Junction (Exeter) shed for services west of Exeter. However, by 1963, particularly after the elimination of steam in Kent a few years earlier, the 'Battle of Britains' were drafted all over the rest of the SR territory. In fact, the collection of photographs featured in this book includes a greater proportion of these over those carrying the West Country names!

We start our journey covering the route of the 'Atlantic Coast Express' in North Devon at Ilfracombe during July 1963 travelling in the 'up' direction to Barnstaple and on to Copplestone. Returning to Barnstaple, a journey over the North Devon & Cornwall Junction Light Railway follows as far as Halwill Junction. Then a journey to Bude is followed by a trip on the North Cornwall line via Launceston as far as west as Delabole. We then follow the Halwill–Okehampton line before venturing westward to Bow then returning to Exeter.

Heading east from Exeter we travel as far as Salisbury, breaking our journey to visit the Seaton and Lyme Regis branches. Now under Western Region control, the days of 'M7s' and Adams Radials had gone with ex-GWR and LMS tanks seeing out the last days of steam before being replaced by diesel multiple-units before closure.

Laurie Golden
October 2014

Ilfracombe was the northernmost destination of the 'Atlantic Coast Express' 226½ miles from Waterloo and the station was perched about 200 feet above sea level. A gradient of 1 in 36 was necessary to lift the line south over the western part of the Exmoor hills and the incline started literally from the end of the platforms. 'Battle of Britain' class 4-6-2 No 34072 *257 Squadron* has just completed the first mile of the climb with the 14.55 Ilfracombe to Exeter local train on Saturday 27th July 1963. On the left can be seen the Lower Slade reservoir which, with the Upper Slade reservoir, supplies Ilfracombe. The steepness of the incline and the curvature is evident in the picture. The Ilfracombe down distant signal post is just visible as the line swings round behind the train warning the driver he had ¾-mile to stop the train as he passed through the Slade Tunnels!

The summit of the line between Barnstaple and Ilfracombe was at Mortehoe & Woolacombe station, some 600 feet above sea level and two miles east of the two villages. Most of the Taunton to Barnstaple trains worked through to Ilfracombe on Saturdays in the summer timetable and the normal formation of five coaches required assistance on the banks. Taunton-bound trains from Ilfracombe were normally provided with a pilot locomotive in front of the train locomotive (usually a GWR 2-6-0) – the pilot locomotive could then be easily detached at Barnstaple Junction. On Saturday 27th July 1963, the normal arrangement is reversed with GWR 2-6-0 No 6346 coupled in front of an unidentified 'N' class Mogul which appears to be doing most of the work. I had travelled down on the forward working of this train having joined it at Dulverton and there was clearly something amiss with No 6346 as it stopped for some time, presumably to raise boiler pressure, at Mortehoe & Woolacombe. The direction of the line at this location is east to west through the cutting below Higher Campscott.

In the early evening of Saturday 27th July 1963, the photographer has crossed to the north side of the line in the cutting below Higher Campscott to photograph the 17.57 Ilfracombe to Taunton train with the pilot 'N' class Mogul, No 31856, coupled outside GWR 2-6-0 6327 and both locomotives (and the SR Mogul's fireman) clearly working hard. The rolling stock of the train shows a variety of coaches, the leading vehicle is a Stanier BCK Corridor Brake Composite appearing to have acquired an overhead electrification warning sign possibly reflecting a recent overhaul.

In the same location below Higher Campscott, the sun has moved round since the Taunton train picture on Saturday 27th July 1963, as 'Battle of Britain' class 4-6-2 No 34075 *264 Squadron* pilots an unidentified 'West Country' class 4-6-2 on the 14.10 Ilfracombe departure. This would combine with Torrington coaches at Barnstaple Junction and Plymouth coaches at Exeter Central. There the restaurant car would be added and a 'Merchant Navy' class 4-6-2 would take the train (now 13 coaches) forward to Waterloo with a scheduled arrival at 20.10. No 34075 retained its original 5,500 gallon tender with the high side raves until withdrawal.

Moving now to the south side of Mortehoe & Woolacombe station, we are near the summit of the 6 miles of 1 in 40 climb from the north bank of the River Taw estuary near Braunton. On Saturday 27th July 1963, an unidentified GWR 2-6-0 at the head of the five coaches of the 13.28 from Taunton has banking assistance from an Ivatt 2-6-2T. The banking locomotive will come off the train at Mortehoe & Woolacombe and return light engine to Braunton. The exhaust from the train locomotive looks as though the fireman is still firing so perhaps the driver has stepped across to observe the person standing in the middle of a field between Bradwell and Willingcott or maybe just to cool off!

Taken just a few hundred yards nearer Ilfracombe from the previous picture on Saturday 27th July 1963, the Ilfracombe portion of the 'Atlantic Coast Express' is hauled by 'Battle of Britain' class 4-6-2 No 34079 *141 Squadron* with assistance in the rear from 'N' class 2-6-0 No 31833. On Saturdays in July and August, the 11.00 departure from Waterloo worked through to Ilfracombe and the restaurant car can be seen as the fourth vehicle in the train. Reaching Barnstaple Junction 211 miles from Waterloo in 4¼ hours to detach the Torrington coaches, it then stopped at all stations to Ilfracombe, the last 15 miles taking 49 minutes.

In another location between Willingcott and Bradwell on Saturday 27th July 1963, the second through train, the 11.45 Waterloo to Ilfracombe, is seen behind 'West Country' class 4-6-2 No 34107 *Blandford Forum*. The banking locomotive is hidden behind the train engine in this picture and was not identified. Again the restaurant car worked through to Ilfracombe and this train was allowed 49 minutes (including stops) between Barnstaple Junction and Ilfracombe. The houses of the settlements of Bradwell and Dean can be seen to the left of the locomotive.

Finally at Willingcott, we see two unidentified Bulleid Pacifics rolling down from their stop at Mortehoe & Woolacombe station with gravity and the 1 in 40 gradient doing most of the work. This 16.50 departure from Ilfracombe will eventually get to Exeter Central at 19.03 stopping at every station except Crediton and Newton St Cyres. The railway formation here has now completely disappeared under the Willingcott Valley Golf Course and cottages but the white house in the background still stands beside the Bradwell Road.

The first 20 miles of the line from Barnstaple to Exeter follows the incised valley of the River Taw. Most of the villages served are on the higher ground which gives the route its unspoiled character, exploited latterly as the Tarka Line. Umberleigh is one of the exceptions being a settlement around the bridge which carried the South Molton to Great Torrington road across the River Taw. 'Battle of Britain' class 4-6-2 No 34079 *141 Squadron* approaches Umberleigh station having just crossed over the River Taw with the 18.15 Ilfracombe to Exeter stopping train on Sunday 28th July 1963. The sidings in the foreground were used by the permanent way department and terminated at the road bridge immediately behind the photographer as seen in the next picture.

An earlier photograph on Sunday 28th July 1963 of the 16.30 Ilfracombe to Exeter train with 'West Country' class 4-6-2 No 34011 *Tavistock* passing through Umberleigh station. From Barnstaple to Umberleigh was double track, so the locomotive will be slowing down to receive the single line tablet for the next section. This train conveyed through carriages from Ilfracombe and Torrington to Waterloo (arrival 22.23) and a buffet car. The multiple single arch over bridges are a feature of this section of the line whose history is long and complicated. It was completed as a broad gauge line and was built and initially operated by Thomas Brassey from 1854 to 1862.

On the single line part of the Exeter to Barnstaple route between Umberleigh and Copplestone, there were crossing places at Portsmouth Arms, King's Nympton, Eggesford, Lapford and Morchard Road. Here 'West Country' class 4-6-2 No 34011 *Tavistock* arrives at King's Nympton with the 10.00 Exeter to Ilfracombe train on Sunday 28th July 1963. The locomotive will have had a four-hour layover at Ilfracombe before returning on the 16.30 departure since it was photographed earlier. The signalman is saving his legs by exchanging the single line tokens in front of the signal box instead of where the locomotive will stop further up the platform. The connection to the goods yard off the down line via the diamond crossing saves a facing point lock as the loops were not signalled for bi-directional working. From opening in 1854 up to 1951 this station was named South Molton Road. In fact Umberleigh was nearer to South Molton than this station and an even closer railway station, with the same name, was opened on the Taunton to Barnstaple line in 1873!

Lapford was the largest settlement between Crediton and Barnstaple having a population of about 500. The village is sited half a mile to the east of the line and several hundred feet above it. The railway here passes from the valley of the River Taw to that of its tributary, the River Yeo until south of Copplestone it crosses the watershed to another River Yeo which is a tributary of the River Exe which it follows to the junction with the Great Western main line and the River Exe valley at Cowley Bridge Junction. Starting with the northern (Barnstaple) end of the station we see 'Battle of Britain' class 4-6-2 No 34070 *Manston* accelerating away from the station with the Ilfracombe and Torrington portion of the 'Atlantic Coast Express' which had left Waterloo at 11.00 on Wednesday 31st July 1963. The destination boards on the roof of each coach are clearly visible. The down starter and up home on an LSWR lattice post are elevated for sighting purposes over the skew road bridge on the A377 visible behind the signal box and an occupation over bridge in the cutting seen to the left of the photographer.

With the signal box and signal visible in the previous picture in the left background, the up platform at Lapford is occupied by 'West Country' class 4-6-2 No 34002 *Salisbury* with the 14.12 Ilfracombe to Exeter train on Wednesday 31st July 1963. The siding in the foreground leads to the Ambrosia dairy and the catch point will be noted as the line this side of the locomotive is the down through line. The North Devon Railway stationmaster houses and railway offices were substantial buildings of varying designs and have generally survived rationalisation of the line.

At the southern (Exeter) end of the station we see an unidentified 'West Country' class 4-6-2 leaving the crossing loop at Lapford on the 13.15 Barnstaple to Exmouth Junction freight service which on Wednesday 31st July 1963 consisted of one box van, two container flats and a brake van. The peculiar island siting of the down platform is clearly visible with only the face to the down line usable. Access to the platform was by stairs from the A377 over bridge that crosses the line at an angle of 45°. As noted in the previous picture, the goods yard was opposite the up platform and station buildings so there was not room there for a down platform. The bridge over the River Yeo in the foreground is of typical construction and was one of the reasons why only unrebuilt Bulleid Light Pacifics were allowed on the Barnstaple line. The lattice signal post in the right foreground carrying the down home signal has a co-acting arm at higher level for sighting over a further road over bridge immediately behind the photographer's right shoulder.

FACING PAGE TOP A mile to the south of Lapford station, 'Battle of Britain' class 4-6-2 34072 *257 Squadron* drifts down the 1 in 110 gradient from Morchard Road and Copplestone with the 16.19 stopping train from Exeter on Wednesday 31st July 1963. The width of the formation shows that it was originally constructed to allow for double track, which the LSWR implemented on some sections of the North Devon line between 1876 and 1891. There is evidence in the right foreground of local burning probably as a result of the fire-throwing for which the Bulleid Pacifics were notorious. However it did help to keep the line side clear of vegetation. This area is now covered with trees, the result of fifty years of reversion to nature.

FACING PAGE BOTTOM At the same site and date as the previous picture but looking now north west towards Lapford station, BR class 3MT 2-6-2T No 82002 has no problem lifting its pick-up freight train up the gradient en route to Exmouth Junction. The three milk tanks would have been collected from Lapford where the Ambrosia plant, which had been built in 1927 and opened in 1928, provided rail traffic until closure in 1970. The site was then used for fertiliser distribution up to the

1990s when it was redeveloped and is now occupied by a removal and storage firm. The seven plank wooden wagon visible behind the vans is of a type that will very soon be withdrawn to be replaced by steel mineral wagons.

ABOVE Copplestone was the last station before the Barnstaple line joins the Crediton to Okehampton line at Coleford Junction. Coleford Junction to Copplestone had been doubled in 1883 so the open door of the signal box means that the signalman has already walked down to the platform to collect the single line tablet from the incoming train. The 12.15 Ilfracombe to Exeter stopping train on Tuesday 30th July 1963 is hauled by 'West Country' class 4-6-2 No 34020 *Seaton* and the normal three coaches have been augmented by a strengthening vehicle whose larger windows and different profile reveal it to be of Maunsell design. The up home signal visible behind the train was one of the few lower quadrant signals remaining on this line and the partially visible goods yard displays the normal collection of a permanent way trolley and various concrete products awaiting use.

The first railway in North Devon was the line along the southern shore of the River Taw from Barnstaple to Fremington Quay that was opened as a horse worked railway in 1848 to allow shipping to avoid the treacherous sands of the estuary. It was eventually joined to the main system and extended through Instow to Bideford in 1855. In the evening light of Saturday 27th July 1963, Ivatt 2-6-2T No 41313 has just left Instow station with the 20.25 Barnstaple to Torrington service. The station buildings and curved awning roof are just visible on the extreme left of the picture as is the flotsam on the beach at the base of the concrete sea wall. The line closed to passengers in 1965 but milk and clay traffic continued to 1982. Following the failure of preservation efforts, the track was lifted in 1985 but happily Instow Signal Box is still with us under the auspices of the Bideford Railway Heritage Centre.

The North Devon & Cornwall line between Torrington and Halwill Junction was opened by the Southern Railway in 1925 as a light railway so all the road crossings were ungated and trains had to observe a 5mph speed restriction. The northern half of the line from Meeth to Torrington was constructed on the formation of a narrow gauge line built to export ball clay. There were three crossing loops at Hatherleigh, Petrockstow and Hole, all of which had manned signal boxes for a service of two passenger and two freight workings a day with a journey time for passengers of just over 1¼ hours for the 20 miles. The town of Hatherleigh with a population of 1,300 was the largest community served but was some two miles from the station. While surviving to be worked by single car diesel units, it closed unsurprisingly to passengers in March 1965. In charge of the one Bulleid corridor brake composite coach on the 08.52 Torrington to Halwill service on Monday 29th July 1963 was Ivatt 2-6-2T 41294. There was plenty of time to take pictures at stations because there was little danger of the train leaving without one of its few passengers.

The line from Torrington was the third arrival at Halwill Junction – one of those country stations which had short periods of intense activity and long periods of slumber! Originally called Beaworthy when the line from Okehampton to Holsworthy was opened in 1879 it was soon renamed Halwill & Beaworthy being about one mile from each of these two small settlements. It became a junction in 1886 with the opening of the first section of the North Cornwall line as far as Launceston. By the time of this July 1964 picture, the BR Standard 4MT 2-6-4Ts had arrived displacing the Southern 2-6-0s and here No 80041 departs with the 10.00 Okehampton to Padstow due to leave Halwill Junction at 10.33. In the down platform behind it is the connection for Bude, in charge of another BR 2-6-4T with its safety valves blowing off, due to leave at 10.40 and in the Torrington bay in the left foreground is an Ivatt 2-6-2T with its single coach due to depart at 10.38. Finally above the Torrington train can be seen the steam from the locomotive of the 08.48 Padstow train shortly to depart at 10.36 for Okehampton.

A little earlier on the same day in July 1964, BR Class 4MT No 80043 is drawing into Halwill Junction with the 09.40 from Bude. The enclosed cabs of these tanks were much appreciated by the footplate crew especially on the exposed part of the North Cornwall line in winter. The train is one of the two coach sets widely used in Devon and Cornwall. The lines are, reading from left to right: to Launceston and Padstow curving away to the west; the goods yard headshunt; the single line to Bude; and the Torrington line with its separate run-round which curves away to the east just beyond the home signal visible in the distance.

ABOVE The next station on the Halwill Junction to Bude line was Dunsland Cross, named after a cross-roads on the Hatherleigh to Holsworthy road about a mile to the north of the station. It was opened in 1879 as a crossing place on the single line between Okehampton and Holsworthy which eventually reached Bude in 1898. 'N' class 2-6-0 No 31855 draws into the down loop with the 03.30 Exmouth Junction to Bude freight just after 10am in July 1964. As noted previously, the 13 ton steel mineral wagon has replaced the wooden wagon and after two oil tanks there is an eclectic collection of vans, the first of which is of Southern origin. The ubiquitous permanent way trolley wheels and body are a reminder of how labour intensive was the maintenance that kept the railway safe to use.

FACING PAGE TOP Following on from the previous picture, the photographer has walked along the up platform to take No 31855 in front of the substantial station building. The driver is seated and leaning back against the cab side sheet presumably deep in conversation with his fireman.

FACING PAGE BOTTOM The arrival of the 09.40 from Bude to Halwill has roused the crew of No 31855 to exchange pleasantries (or more likely insults!) with the driver of the BR Class 4MT 2-6-4T working bunker first. The fireman can be seen leaning out to exchange single line tablets with the signalman. Judging by the chimney of No 31855, the crew have the blower on, ready to move off as soon as they have the tablet for the next section to Holsworthy.

Moving now to the North Cornwall line to Launceston and Wadebridge, Tower Hill station was opened in 1886 nine miles from Halwill Junction and five miles from Launceston. On Monday 29th July 1963, a few passengers disembark from the 10.00 Okehampton to Padstow train hauled by 'N' class 2-6-0 No 31845. The passing loop here had been removed as early as 1920 but was restored in 1943 to handle heavy wartime traffic in the form of 40 van ammunition trains prior to the D-Day invasion. Because of the length of the loop, it was retained for the heavy holiday traffic of the 1950s but in early 1964 was taken out of use. After closure of the line in 1966, the substantial station house was demolished.

'Battle of Britain' class 4-6-2 No 34075 *264 Squadron* is about 1½ miles east of Launceston as it drops down into the valley of the River Tamar with the 15.32 all stations Okehampton to Wadebridge in July 1964. The 'Atlantic Coast Express' portion for Padstow only stopped at principal stations so this train provided connections for the other intermediate stations. It will be noted that the overbridge and cutting have been constructed for double track although it only ever carried a single track.

Launceston was first served by a broad gauge branch from Plymouth and Tavistock that was opened in 1865, the line from Halwill Junction arriving in 1886. The two stations were next to each other and an early form of co-operation was a 1916 signal box on the LSWR station that had two frames, one for the LSWR and the other for the Great Western. However the lines were not connected until September 1943 when fears of disruption of routes to Plymouth by bombing meant new connections here and at St Budeaux and restoration of an earlier connection at Lydford. From 1952 all passenger trains used the LSWR platforms and the GWR station was devoted to goods traffic. On Monday 29th July 1963, 'N' class No 31836 is shunting the Wadebridge to Exmouth Junction freight train having detached the brake van. To the right of the locomotive can be seen the lower quadrant down home signal on the connection between the ex GWR and Southern lines from which passenger services had been withdrawn the previous December.

Viewed from the end of the down platform at Launceston station, 'Battle of Britain' class 4-6-2 No 34080 *74 Squadron* arrives on Monday 29th July 1963 with the 15.32 Okehampton to Wadebridge stopping train described earlier. The up starting signal gives equal status to the left hand route over the connection to the GWR for Plymouth trains and the right hand route on the LSWR line to Halwill Junction. Immediately behind the rail-built signal post is a wooden 'garage' for a motorised permanent way trolley and the ganger has left his ballast fork and key hammer leaning against it. Between the signal and the locomotive can be seen the water tower (painted in WR brown and cream) and stone-built locomotive shed which was used by both companies from the 1940s.

ABOVE 'N' class 2-6-0 No 31843 is working the 13.00 Padstow to Okehampton train on Monday 29th July 1963 as it approaches Launceston on the down gradient crossing the two arch bridge over the River Kensey. 2½ miles of the trackbed west from Launceston to Newmills, including the stretch in this view, are now the home of the Launceston Steam Railway which operates on track of gauge 1ft 11½in and was opened in 1983.

.

FACING PAGE TOP The North Cornwall Railway west of Launceston was opened gradually, the first section of seven miles from Launceston to Tresmeer being opened in July 1892 with an intermediate crossing place at Egloskerry but the station at Egloskerry was not opened until October 1892. 'N' class 2-6-0 No 31859 is in charge of the 13.00 Padstow to Okehampton in July 1964 making a spirited departure from the station. By this time most of these trains were due to be worked by BR class 4MT 2-6-4Ts and the usual Maunsell two-coach set has been replaced by more modern but less clean stock!

FACING PAGE BOTTOM The station buildings at Egloskerry are seen in the background as 'Battle of Britain' class 4-6-2 No 34075 *264 Squadron* passes through with the 09.33 Padstow portion of the 'Atlantic Coast Express' on Tuesday 30th July 1963. This will join the Bude coaches at Halwill Junction and the Plymouth coaches at Okehampton giving an arrival at Waterloo at 15.32. The signalman holds the single line tablet for the Egloskerry to Launceston section and the fireman will be leaning out with the Tresmeer to Egloskerry tablet bracing himself against the tender to make the exchange.

ABOVE 'Battle of Britain' class 4-6-2 No 34066 *Spitfire* swings round the curve half a mile to the east of Tresmeer station with the Padstow portion of the 'Atlantic Coast Express' in July 1964. The train is just passing milepost 231¼ from Waterloo, which has taken five hours. The last 30 miles to Padstow is scheduled to take another hour. The open and generally sparsely inhabited nature of this part of North Cornwall is evident so once the through rail traffic ceased the line was totally uneconomic. The buildings of the hamlet of Westcott can be seen above the rear of the train.

FACING PAGE TOP 'Battle of Britain' class 4-6-2 No 34080 *74 Squadron* was apparently rostered to work the up 08.40 Padstow to Exeter and the return down 16.46 Exeter to Padstow stopping trains in the week commencing Monday 29th July 1963. Here on Tuesday 30th July 1963 No 34080 basks in the evening sun at Tresmeer waiting for the 18.00 Padstow train to arrive and surrender the single line tablet. The height of the up starting signal should be noted to allow it to be sighted under the road bridge. The village of Tresmeer was over a mile away to

the south east but the name of the locality of the station (Splatt) must have been deemed inappropriate for a railway station!

FACING PAGE BOTTOM The previous day, Monday 29th July 1963, No 34080 was photographed at Camelford on the up working. Having left Padstow an hour before the 'Atlantic Coast Express', it stopped at all stations except Newton St Cyres, and arrived at Exeter Central 14 minutes before the express. However that did allow passengers to make an onward connection if the express did not stop at their station. Of particular interest is the motorised permanent way trolley visible in the down platform awaiting the single line tablet for the section to Delabole. Many of these trollies were made by Wickham and kept in 'garages' such as the one seen at Launceston. Some used a JAP vee-twin engine and were light enough to be lifted off the line by a line gang of four permanent way men. On the trollies being scrapped they were much sought after for the engines by restorers of Morgan three-wheeler cars.

ABOVE Just to the west of Delabole station with the houses on Westdown Road visible in the background, the up late afternoon freight from Wadebridge is seen on Monday 29th July 1963. In charge is 'N' class 2-6-0 No 31841 and, with the exception of two standard vans, each vehicle is different. The 13-ton mineral wagon, container on a flat wagon and the sloped side wagon and brake van would make this an interesting train to model.

FACING PAGE TOP 'Battle of Britain' class 4-6-2 No 34066 *Spitfire* arrives at Delabole on Monday 29th July 1963 with the stopping train that followed the down 'Atlantic Coast Express' from Okehampton to Wadebridge. In the background behind the rear coach can be seen 'N' class 2-6-0 in the goods yard head shunt which will follow the passenger train once it has reached the next crossing station at Port Isaac Road. The slate-hung walls and the roofing of the station building would presumably have come from the Delabole slate quarry situated immediately to the east of the station.

FACING PAGE BOTTOM Having now received the single line tablet and the starting signal, 'N' class 2-6-0 No 31837 has drawn its train forward and sets off for Port Isaac Road, the next station on the way to Wadebridge, on Monday 29th July 1963. Once again an eclectic variety of rolling stock has been assembled with goods vans of BR, LMS and Southern origin, an open wagon and brake van. On the right can be seen a fairly new goods van adjacent to the store and beyond it the edge of the great Delabole slate quarry which is over 400 feet deep and 1½ miles in circumference. Mechanisation means that five men achieve the same slate-production rate of 100 tons per day now rather than 1,000 employed in the mid 19th century.

ABOVE The final view of Delabole on Monday 29th July 1963 shows the arrival of the 18.20 Padstow to Okehampton service with the signalman and the fireman of 'N' class 2-6-0 No 31844 demonstrating how to exchange single line tablets. The station master's wife certainly believes in Monday being washing day and one presumes the footplate staff will take due care not to cause her to have to re-wash anything! Bill and I caught this train to Otterham, where we made the mile-long trek on a path through wheat fields to the youth hostel in the village, providing supper for the resident horseflies on the way!

FACING PAGE TOP Up to the early 1960s, the LSWR 'T9' 4-4-0s had been the normal motive power for most of the local passenger services west of Okehampton. The Railway Correspondence & Travel Society and Plymouth Railway Circle organised a special train on 27th April 1963 from Exeter Central to Padstow and back. Motive power was 'T9' No 120 which had been given a heavy casual repair at Eastleigh in March 1962 and restored to LSWR livery and its Urie condition

as first superheated. It continued in revenue earning service until October 1963 and was preserved being currently at the Bodmin & Wenford Railway. I therefore could not resist the opportunity to travel from Surbiton to Otterham to photograph the special on its old stamping ground, unfortunately in gloomy weather.

FACING PAGE BOTTOM Between Halwill Junction and Okehampton, the only crossing place was at Ashbury some two miles south west of the church and settlement of that name. At various times after opening of the line in 1879 it had been called Ashbury and North Lew (Northlew is a village 2½ miles away) but had reverted to Ashbury after 1948. In July 1964, 'Battle of Britain' class 4-6-2 34066 *Spitfire* exchanges single line tokens on the up working of the Padstow and Bude portions of the 'Atlantic Coast Express'. The station building on the down platform survives as a private dwelling but the up platform shelter and signal box have been demolished.

On the main Okehampton to Plymouth line, 'N' class 2-6-0 No 31844 has just passed Meldon Junction on Tuesday 30th July 1963 with the 09.50 from Plymouth to Okehampton which connected with the 08.48 from Padstow for onward travel to Exeter. The removed arm on the up signal referred to entry to the up refuge siding which is seen in the title page picture and the down splitting signal for Meldon Junction can be seen to the left. Just a mile beyond Meldon Junction the line reaches an altitude of 950 feet above sea level which was the highest point on the Southern Railway system.

By July 1964 when this picture was taken, most services on the Exeter to Okehampton to Plymouth line had become diesel-hauled. One regular exception, which remained steam-hauled, was the daily through train that ran each way between Plymouth and Brighton. Here the Plymouth to Brighton train is seen passing Bridestowe hauled by 'West Country' class 4-6-2 No 34106 *Lydford* heading for the next station Okehampton. As the previous station it had passed through was Lydford, it is nearly a case of 'snap' as far as the locomotive and station name are concerned!

In the cutting between Meldon Junction and Meldon Viaduct, 'Battle of Britain' class 4-6-2 No 34066 *Spitfire* is seen on Tuesday 30th July 1963 with the 11.05 Plymouth Friary to Yeoford freight. Once again there is a mixture of goods vans of various origins and steel mineral wagons on the train. No 34066 went into Eastleigh for a Light Intermediate repair in January 1964 that may account for its promotion from freight and stopping passenger duties in July 1963 to express passenger duties in July 1964.

Rebuilt 'Battle of Britain' class 4-6-2 No 34060 *25 Squadron* swings across Meldon Viaduct with the up Plymouth to Brighton service slowing down for its stop at Okehampton on Tuesday 30th July 1963. No 34060 was an Exmouth Junction locomotive from 1951 to November 1963 and had been rebuilt in October and November 1960. Rebuilt Bulleid Light Pacifics were permitted to run to Plymouth but not to Barnstaple or Halwill Junction. The photographer is standing at the west end of the Meldon Quarry site and after the line beyond the viaduct was closed, one line remained on the up side as a head shunt for the quarry until 1990.

Meldon Viaduct takes the railway 150ft above the Okement Valley on a rising down gradient of 1 in 77 and a 30 chain radius. Viewed from below the two stages of its construction become clearer. When first opened in 1874 for the line to Lydford it was for a single track only. In 1878 the line was doubled by erecting a second viaduct on the south side, linked by extending the deck and bracing the tops of the trestles. The exposed position of the viaduct and the forces exerted upon it by trains travelling around the curve resulted in speed and weight restrictions being imposed. In 1938 braces were added between the lower end of the older trestles and in 1944, in order to allow heavy wartime traffic, the outer trestle legs were weighted with additional concrete to resist uplift. The viaduct was further strengthened between 1959 and 1960 with the inner trestle legs being weighted and the up line trestle bracing being replaced with stronger section members. In this July 1964 picture, a BR Class 4MT 2-6-4T is seen on the up girders with the 15.35 Bude to Okehampton service. Since 1990 it has been scheduled as an ancient monument and can be walked or cycled over.

Immediately to the east of Meldon Viaduct is Meldon Quarry which provided granite ballast for all the Southern Railway replacing less satisfactory materials like shingle. To shunt wagons under the loading hoppers, a locomotive was allocated to the small shed seen at the right of this picture. For many years this duty was carried out by an Adams 'G6' 0-6-0T but from 1962, 'USA' class 0-6-0T No 30062 which was no longer needed at Southampton Docks was used, having been renumbered DS234 to signify it was no longer on the capital inventory. This locomotive was built by the Vulcan Iron works, Wilkes Barre, Pennsylvania in 1942 and came into service on the Southern Railway in 1947.

Looking west from the down platform at Okehampton station, BR Class 5MT 4-6-0 No 73161 is seen with the late afternoon freight from Plymouth Friary to Exeter in July 1964 which consists of vans and five plank open wagons. The station at Okehampton is some way above the town and the signal box on the right is twice as high at the back as the front. The line continues to climb at 1 in 77 in the Plymouth direction as is evident from the goods vans which are to be collected by this train which can be seen on the level sidings in the distance leading to the loading dock for military vehicles. The co-acting arms on the down starting signal seen on the left were for sighting purposes over the station footbridge between the platforms behind the photographer. The design of the signal box followed closely that of the LSWR Type 4 signal boxes but was not built until 1935. Happily much of this infrastructure is still with us today.

'Battle of Britain' class 4-6-2 No 34066 *Spitfire* approaches Okehampton passing the up advanced starter with the Padstow and Bude portion of the 'Atlantic Coast Express' in July 1964. As noted previously, No 34066 was a regular performer on this train in its last summer and in September 1964 was transferred from Exmouth Junction to Salisbury. Just to the left of the signal arm can be seen the arches of the viaduct over the East Okement River where the final climb at 1 in 77 resumes to the summit beyond Meldon Junction. To the right of the down distant signal can be seen the buffer stop of the down sidings which are level with the station, enabling appreciation of the steepness of the gradient.

There was sufficient time after the previous picture to walk the length of Okehampton station to take 'Battle of Britain' class 4-6-2 No 34066 *Spitfire* on the 'Atlantic Coast Express' before its departure for Halwill Junction and Padstow in July 1964. This view illustrates the signal box and footbridge referred to in earlier pictures. In the platform on the right is the Plymouth connection, now in charge of a North British Type 2 diesel-hydraulic since the lines west of Exeter were transferred to the Western Region in January 1964. Although this platform had a run-round connection to the down main, it could only be used as a bay platform for passenger trains leaving in the Plymouth direction. To the right of the diesel can just be seen the edge of the goods shed.

BR Class 5MT 4-6-0 No 73161, photographed earlier approaching Okehampton station, has now collected the vans from the up sidings and makes its way in the Coleford Junction direction on a late afternoon in July 1964. The second vehicle in the train is one of the 25-ton bogie brake vans generally known as the 'Queen Marys'. The first batch were rebuilds in 1933 of redundant LBSC AC electric motor luggage vans. These were so successful that a further batch of 25 were authorised in 1935. While they were not confined to Meldon Quarry ballast trains, one would expect their additional weight and braking power to be useful on such heavy trains.

Sampford Courtenay lies between the valleys of the Rivers Taw and Okement and the easing to 1 in 250 through the station provides a respite on the 1 in 76 ruling gradient as the line climbs over the north west edge of Dartmoor. 'West Country' class 4-6-2 No 34002 *Salisbury* is making good progress with the Brighton to Plymouth train on a late afternoon in July 1964 and the fireman is able to take a breather. With only five trains each way a day, the staff have plenty of time to keep everything neat and tidy on the station from the candy-twist lamp standards to the well tended bushes.

The station houses at Bow and North Tawton were elegant gabled structures with gothic freestone surrounds to their round-headed windows. The north elevation can be glimpsed on the left of this picture as 'Battle of Britain' class 4-6-2 *Spitfire* is seen on its regular 'Atlantic Coast Express' duty in July 1964, in this case the up working which left Padstow at 09.33. The difference in height between the original platforms immediately in front of the station building and the cast concrete faced extensions at either end is very obvious. Why the platforms needed to be extended is not clear as the original platform would accommodate a four-coach train. The signal box was still in place but had closed in January 1964 and was of typical LSWR design with a local stone base, however the upper woodwork had been replaced by brick.

On Wednesday 31st July 1963, 'Battle of Britain' class 4-6-2 No 34070 *Manston* works the up Padstow portion of the 'Atlantic Coast Express' round the curve towards Coleford Junction from Bow. Having left Padstow at 9.33, it is due to arrive at Exeter Central at 12.12. As we have already seen No 34070 was then used on the Ilfracombe portion of the down 'Atlantic Coast Express' which was due to leave Exeter at 14.04 giving two hours for turning and servicing. The exposed rock on the right shows that the underlying rock is red sandstone that is so characteristic of the area and the geological name for this series of rocks is Devonian. In the foreground can be seen the signal wires from Coleford Junction signal box to the up distant signal which was 1,750 yards from the junction. The coaches appear to be a scratch set which may explain the all 1st class coach in the centre rather than the normal composite 1st/3rd.

Twenty minutes earlier than the 'Atlantic Coast Express', the 08.30 from Padstow on Wednesday 31st July 1963 passes under the minor road overbridge a mile west of Coleford Junction with 'Battle of Britain' class 4-6-2 No 34066 *Spitfire* at the head of the normal formation of a four-wheeled goods van and a two coach set. As noted previously, under the Southern Railway pattern of services this train provided an onward connection from intermediate stations to the 'Atlantic Coast Express' at Exeter. The bridge in the background was the first on the Devon and Cornwall line to Okehampton and displays a different architectural style from the multiple single arch over bridges on the original North Deveon line to Barnstaple. In the foreground it will be noted that the bullhead rail has been replaced by heavier flat-bottom rail reflecting continuing investment to carry the output of Meldon Quarry.

ABOVE Starting our journey east from Exeter in July 1964, the first station seen is that at Whimple, 8½ miles from Exeter Central. This was one of the original stations on the Exeter Extension of the Salisbury and Yeovil Railway opened in 1860 and the original low platforms that could accommodate four coaches were extended in the Salisbury direction by concrete platforms to the modern height. 'Merchant Navy' class 4-6-2 No 35025 *Brocklebank Line* passes with the weekday 15.00 Waterloo to Plymouth train with the locomotive smokebox showing signs of overheating due to accumulation of char. For many years there was considerable goods traffic at this station associated with the cider factory of Whiteway's, reflecting the local apple orchards. The station was retained as an unstaffed halt using the down platform after the singling of the line in 1967. The inconvenience of using the footbridge was ended when the station was reconstructed and the line slewed to the up platform in 1993.

FACING PAGE TOP The next station towards Salisbury was opened as Feniton in 1860, being renamed Ottery Road in 1861, Ottery St Mary in 1868 and Sidmouth Junction when the branch line to Sidmouth via Tipton St Johns was opened in 1874. With the rationalisation of the line between Salisbury and Exeter in 1967, Sidmouth Junction was closed but re-opened as Feniton in 1971. The line between Tipton St Johns and Exmouth Junction was completed in 1907 and a number of holiday trains originating at Exmouth, Littleham and Sidmouth were routed via Sidmouth Junction. Here BR Class 3MT 2-6-2Ts Nos 82033 and 82035 approach Sidmouth Junction on the single line from Ottery St Mary with the home signal indicating their route into the down main platform rather than the down bay. Their train consists of the Saturdays only 09.32 from Sidmouth and 08.55 from Exmouth (which was only advertised in the public timetable from Littleham, the first station between Exmouth and Budleigh Salterton, at 09.10). The two trains combined at Tipton St Johns and provided through carriages to Waterloo.

FACING PAGE BOTTOM The two tanks having arrived on the down main line, 'West Country' class 4-6-2 No 34106 *Lydford* has arrived on the up main having left at Exeter Central at 09.30. Drawing forward, No 34106 sets back to collect the Sidmouth and Exmouth coaches in the down platform. Only 11 minutes was allowed for this manoeuvre and the signal box diagram shows no facing point locks on this crossover so an Inspector would have been present to 'clip' the crossover points to prevent them moving under a train with passengers.

Having passed through Sidmouth Junction and crossed the River Otter viaduct, the climb to Honiton Tunnel begins. For five miles the ruling gradient is 1 in 100 easing to 1 in 300 through Honiton station. 'Merchant Navy' class 4-6-2 No 35013 *Blue Funnel* is one mile into this hard work with the 10 coaches of the 08.25 Plymouth to Waterloo on a Saturday in July 1964. The attractive brickwork of the original under bridge survives today albeit with safety hand rails added to the top of the walls. In the background the A30 trunk road has already been made into a dual carriageway but it would be another two years before the by-pass would be opened, removing the notorious bottleneck of Honiton for holiday road traffic.

Moving a short way back towards Sidmouth Junction, we see the following all stations Saturdays only 10.33 Exeter to Salisbury hauled by 'Battle of Britain' class 4-6-2 No 34080 *74 Squadron* in July 1964. The A30 in the background has reverted to single carriageway with traditional hedgerows and a few cars can be seen to the left of the picture on the B road which passes under the line here. Since the previous year when No 34080 was working on the North Cornwall line, it now appears to be on the Salisbury workings from Exmouth Junction which harder work may account for the evidence on the smokebox door of ash and char accumulation leading to combustion and burning of the paintwork.

ABOVE Between 1960 and 1964, day car/carrier services were operated between Surbiton and Okehampton on weekdays and Saturdays (Waterloo and Exeter Central on Sundays). The 185 miles were covered in 4½ hours at a fare of £12 single and £20 return for driver and car and passengers at £2 6s 6d (£2.325p) single or £4 13s 0d (£4.65p) return. With petrol at 5s 0d (25p) per gallon this represented a large premium on the cost of fuel but a considerable saving in time and effort. Here the down working (08.03 Surbiton to 12.20 Okehampton) is seen descending Honiton bank with 'Merchant Navy' class 4-6-2 No 35017 *Belgian Marine*. The normal formation was eight Covered Carriage Trucks that allowed end loading of the cars and three passenger carriages (including a restaurant car). Passengers boarded the coaches by step-ladder from the goods yard at Surbiton and not from the platform.

FACING PAGE TOP The last mile of the east-bound bank steepened to 1 in 90 from Honiton station to the summit at Milepost 153½ just to the west of Honiton Tunnel. The fireman

of 'West Country' class 4-6-2 No 34002 *Salisbury* is taking a rest having done the hard work to get the Saturday only 11.10 Plymouth to Brighton this far in July 1964. With through coaches to Portsmouth and Southsea, the obvious clientele were Royal Navy personnel that may account for the three coaches with First Class accommodation for officers!

FACING PAGE BOTTOM Turning to take the going away shot of the Plymouth to Brighton, an unidentified 'Battle of Britain' class 4-6-2 emerges from Honiton Tunnel with 09.00 Waterloo to Sidmouth and Exmouth. As seen previously the train would be worked from Sidmouth Junction to Tipton St Johns by two BR or Ivatt 2-6-2Ts where it would divide into Sidmouth and Exmouth portions. The point onto the Sidmouth Branch from the down platform was fitted with a facing point lock for this movement. This departure was scheduled at 13.10 while the Pacific would already be on its way to Exmouth Junction shed as a light engine movement.

Honiton Tunnel was 1,353 yards long at a gradient of 1 in 132 against west-bound trains. This easing from the ruling gradient of 1 in 80 for the four miles from Seaton Junction was much appreciated by the footplate crew on down trains. However 'Battle of Britain' class No 34059 *Sir Archibald Sinclair* has only a lightweight train on the 13.10 Exeter to Yeovil Junction as it emerges from the eastern portal of the tunnel. On weekdays this train could get to Yeovil Junction at 14.45 but on Summer Saturdays in July 1964, it had to wait at Chard Junction from 14.17 to 14.56 to allow the 12.00 Ilfracombe and up 'Atlantic Coast Express' to pass and so the arrival at Yeovil Junction was not until 15.22. The two leading coaches are GWR auto-coaches which are probably being worked back to Yeovil following routine maintenance at Exeter.

At the eastern portal of Honiton Tunnel, the first part of the 'Atlantic Coast Express' (10.35 Waterloo to Padstow and Bude) is seen hauled by 'West Country' class 4-6-2 No 34026 *Yes Tor*. The coal in the tender is out of sight but some of the overspill can be seen behind the bunker. The telephone cabinet in the foreground enabled footplate crew of stalled locomotives to communicate with the signalmen. On the down side of the line just before the tunnel can be seen the valve house for the pipe work of a water supply from natural springs in the ground above. This fed by gravity (with a 250ft head) the signal box, railway cottages and the Express Dairy factory at Seaton Junction.

Moving a few hundred yards downhill, 'West Country' class 4-6-2 No 34023 *Blackmore Vale* accelerates from the tunnel with the up 'Atlantic Coast Express' with portions from Padstow (11.00 departure) and Bude (11.45 departure). No 34023 was one of two unrebuilt Bulleid Pacifics surviving in July 1967 and was preserved by the Bulleid Society from withdrawal. Currently sporting the original number and name 21C123 *Blackmoor Vale*, the locomotive is based on the Bluebell Railway but not currently in service.

'West Country' class 4-6-2 No 34091 *Weymouth* is well in control near the summit of Honiton Bank with the 10.15 Waterloo to Ilfracombe and Torrington. The significance of the oil lamp on the left front lower lamp iron is not known - perhaps left there when working light engine from Nine Elms to Waterloo to couple onto the train? The cleanness of the locomotive's exhaust when working hard is remarkable and may speak as much of the ambient temperature as the efficiency of combustion and steam use.

FACING PAGE TOP 'Merchant Navy' class 4-6-2 No 35026 *Lamport & Holt Line* has steam to spare as it restarts the 13 coaches of the Ilfracombe portion of the 'Atlantic Coast Express' (11.00 from Waterloo) from a signal check at Honiton Incline Box. The locomotive is just about to pass under the road overbridge about half a mile from the eastern entrance of Honiton Tunnel and managed to get the heavy train on the move without any trace of slipping on the 1 in 80 gradient. The driver and fireman are looking back along the train, perhaps to make sure they have a complete train!

FACING PAGE BOTTOM It was not unusual to find a BR Class 5MT 4-6-0 pressed into service on summer Saturdays working between Exeter and Waterloo on trains booked for a 'Merchant Navy' pacific. Here an unidentified member of the class approaches Seaton Junction with the 11.00 Padstow to Waterloo with the safety valves lifting as gravity has done the work to accelerate the train down the bank. The advanced starting signals for the local and through lines on the gantry that frames the train were lower quadrant LSWR arms until at least 1959.

ABOVE The 11.00 Padstow to Waterloo was followed by the 11.48 Plymouth to Waterloo which was all stations to Exeter and then principal stations to Waterloo, the 'Merchant Navy' class 4-6-2 No 35017 *Belgian Marine* and buffet car coming on at Exeter. No 35017 has already been seen on the down car carrier train and would have had three hours to be serviced at Exmouth Junction shed before coming onto this train for a 14.30 departure. As No 35017 pulls away from its station stop at Seaton Junction past the co-acting arms of the starting signals, the driver has the steam sanding on and steam to spare. This view from the road overbridge at the east of the station shows the extent of the 1927/1928 rebuilding which retained the original station building on the up side but added separate local and through roads and the famous up 'sky' co-acting signals installed for sighting purposes for trains coming at high speed down the bank. Under the footbridge and over the rear coaches of the train can be seen milk tank wagons for the milk depot and creamery visible to the right of the station building.

The Seaton branch platform at Seaton Junction was built in 1927/1928 prior to which branch trains had to draw past the station and reverse into a bay platform on the down side. Under the concrete footbridge can be seen the new signal box provided for the rebuilt station. After the lines were transferred to the Western Region in 1963, auto fitted GWR pannier tanks worked the branch until diesel multiple units took over in November 1963. However a crisis in diesel multiple unit availability in February 1965 meant that both the Seaton and Lyme Regis branches returned to steam operation. '14xx' class 0-4-2T Nos 1442 and 1450 were transferred from Yeovil to Exmouth Junction on 7th February 1965 to cover the Seaton branch. Presumably because it would have been uncomfortable for the crews to work bunker first down the main line for 50 miles, both locomotives were turned together on the turntable at Yeovil Junction to run down chimney first. Exmouth Junction must have then turned No 1442 as in February and March 1965 the locomotive faced toward Seaton whereas No 1450 retained the traditional direction, facing towards Seaton Junction. However the GWR auto-coach had the driver end towards Seaton Junction whereas before 1963 the driver end faced Seaton. Here we see No 1442 leaving Seaton Junction for Seaton with the 11.50 service on Saturday 27th February 1965.

'14xx' class 0-4-2T No 1442 is seen on the previous 10.25 from Seaton Junction to Seaton on Saturday 27th February 1965 at Colyford, one of the two intermediate stations. The passenger facilities here consisted of a concrete hut that can just be seen behind the end of the coach. The crossing keeper can be seen on the right, having unlocked the level crossing and wicket gates at the two-lever ground frame, going to open the gates to road traffic on the A3052 Exeter to Lyme Regis road. The trackbed of the branch here was given a new use when the miniature electric trams were transferred from Eastbourne and the Seaton & District Electric Tramway was opened in August 1970 between a new station in Seaton via Colyford to Colyton station.

Having arrived at Seaton on Saturday 27th February 1965 at the end of its 10 minute journey for the four miles from Seaton Junction, '14xx' class 0-4-2T 1442 has shunted onto the run-round loop that led to the water column and coaling facilities. The GWR used a mechanical system to transmit the regulator motion from the driving end of the trailer to the footplate as opposed to the Southern Railway system that used compressed air from a Westinghouse pump on the locomotive. It was more work therefore to uncouple locomotive and trailer on the GWR system and was avoided unless necessary. It will also be noted that the GWR practice is being followed of leaving the lamp on the centre buffer beam lamp iron whether propelling or hauling. Strictly speaking the lamp should be on the lamp iron at the top of the smokebox when at the head of a stopping passenger train. The concrete platforms and fence posts and the substantial starting signal gantry all date from the rebuilding of Seaton station in 1936.

Finally looking from the eastern Axmouth side of the tidal estuary of the River Axe, we see '14xx' 0-4-2T No 1442 propelling its trailer towards Seaton Junction on the 10.40 from Seaton on Saturday 27th February 1965. There are no passengers visible on the train and the last passenger train in 1966 had only 12 passengers. As noted above this section of the trackbed is now used by the 2ft 9in gauge trams of the Seaton & District Electric Tramway.

ABOVE Axminster station was opened in 1860 and only became a junction in 1903 when the light railway to Lyme Regis was opened. The impressive station building on the down platform was designed by Sir William Tite and is happily still with us today. In July 1964 BR Class 5MT No 73171 has just received the right away to restart the 11.30 Brighton to Plymouth train from its 15.32 stop. The lower of the two co-acting arms of the down starting signal can be seen on the right with the upper arm providing sighting for down trains over the station footbridge. The Lyme Regis trains left from a bay on the up platform to the left of the picture. There is at least one trolley of 'Passenger Luggage in Advance' to be transferred between branch and main line trains.

FACING PAGE TOP Similarly to the Seaton branch, there was a resumption of steam operation in February and early March 1965 until the closure of the Halwill to Torrington line released single car diesel units. On Saturday 27th February 1965, the 13.42 service to Lyme Regis is operated by Ivatt Class 2MT No 41216 and a Western Region auto-coach. Seen here climbing away from Axminster having crossed over the main line, No 41216 was not fitted for push-pull working and so had to run round the coach at both Axminster and Lyme Regis.

FACING PAGE BOTTOM There was no difficulty in outpacing the train by car to be able to take the same train at the intermediate station of Combpyne on Saturday 27th February 1965. It will be noted that the locomotive carries no headlamp perhaps because of the Southern Railway practice of using a white circular board during daylight hours. Originally Combpyne was a crossing place, however it was rationalised to a siding as early as 1921 and the siding was used for a camping coach from the 1940s. One writer has remarked that the campers were a hardy breed as the coaches had no heating or running water. As with the station house supply, delivery was by train with the water carried in milk churns up until closure in November 1965.

ABOVE Just south of the hamlet of Winsham between Chard Junction and Crewkerne, 'Merchant Navy' class 4-6-2 No 35013 *Blue Funnel* rolls down the 1 in 200 from Hewish summit with the 15.35 Templecombe to Exeter stopping train in July 1964. No 35013 would have come off the 08.25 Plymouth to Waterloo train having reached Salisbury and have two hours to turn and water before working light engine from Salisbury to Templecombe. The bridge in the foreground over the Chard to Broadwindsor road is of limited 13 ft 6in clearance that may account for it being a girder span rather than the brick arches characteristic of other under-structures.

FACING PAGE TOP 'U' class 2-6-0 No 31798 passes under the A37 Yeovil to Dorchester road with the 13.25 Yeovil Town to Exeter local train in July 1964. Having just left Yeovil Junction it will make its way slowly west including nearly an hour pause

at Seaton Junction before eventually getting to Exeter Central at 15.39. The train provided local connections from the 11.15 Waterloo to Padstow and Bude that left Yeovil Junction at 13.35, ten minutes before this train. Unusually for Southern Railway locomotives, the driver of the Maunsell Mogul was on the right side of the footplate as the reach rod from the cab to the valve gear shows.

FACING PAGE BOTTOM 'Merchant Navy' class 4-6-2 No 35006 *Peninsular & Oriental S.N. Co.* has just restarted after stopping at Yeovil Junction in July 1964 and, with only seven coaches on the 13.00 Waterloo to Plymouth and Ilfracombe, is not unduly taxed by the steepening gradient as it passes the village of Stoford. The up home signals for Yeovil Junction West or A signal box can be seen as the line curves round behind the train.

ABOVE 'West Country' class 4-6-2 No 34005 *Barnstaple* is fresh from overhaul and has been rostered by Salisbury shed for the 09.00 Waterloo to Plymouth semi-fast train, seen here starting from Yeovil Junction station in July 1964. No 34005 was the first of the Bulleid Light Pacifics to be rebuilt in June 1957. It went into Eastleigh for a Light Intermediate overhaul on 29th April 1964 and only emerged on 27th July 1964 after the work was upgraded to a Heavy Intermediate overhaul. The station had been completely reconstructed in 1908 with through lines and two island platforms. The platform face on the right was a bay platform and could only be used by down passenger train departures.

FACING PAGE TOP Another view from the west end of Yeovil Junction, BR Class 4MT 2-6-0 No 76007 and its three-coach set form the 15.35 Templecombe to Exeter stopping train and await the right away having the down local starting signal off. The down main starting signal is hidden by the horizontal girder of the signal gantry. Sighting problems for up and down trains caused by the substantial covered footbridge caused the installation of a repeating banner signal on the footbridge for the up starter and a repeating banner signal on the gantry of the up starting signals for the down main starter. The red brick building to the right of the locomotive was used by the Engineer's Department but was formerly the part of the GWR Clifton Maybank goods station until 1937.

FACING PAGE BOTTOM Moving now to the east end of the down platform of Yeovil Junction station, 'Battle of Britain' class 4-6-2 No 34079 *141 Squadron* waits to depart with the Sundays only 16.00 train which was all stations to Salisbury and then fast to Waterloo. The major town of Yeovil was some 1½ miles north of the Junction station and there was a regular shuttle service between Yeovil Town and Yeovil Junction stations. The train seen here had left Yeovil Town at 15.50 with the locomotive hauling the train tender first and No 34079 would have run round at the Junction before departure.

Viewed from the cattle dock to the north of the up platform at Yeovil Junction, it is just before 18.30 on a summer Saturday in July 1964 and the early evening sun has moved round to reflect off the 'air smoothed' casing of 'Battle of Britain' class 4-6-2 No 34080 *74 Squadron* which is in charge of the 16.42 Exeter to Salisbury all stations stopping train. After the rationalisation of the Salisbury to Exeter line in 1967, the down platform, and its buildings whose chimney stacks are visible over the first coach of the train, was abandoned and this up platform was retained with the footbridge truncated.

The ballast shoulder of the up line is visible on the left edge of this picture together with the Yeovil Junction East or B signal box which controlled the junction with the line that swung north to Yeovil Town. 'Battle of Britain' class 4-6-2 No 34079 *141 Squadron* had left Exeter Central at 13.10 on a Summer Saturday in July 1964 which as noted earlier (page 60) had paused at Chard Junction to allow the through expresses to pass. This train is en route to Yeovil Town where No 34079 would go onto the shed to be serviced and turned. The engineer's wagon visible in front of the locomotive was on one of the nearly two miles of sidings at Yeovil Junction indicating its importance as an interchange facility with the GWR as well as a marshalling point for freight services on the Southern line.

The Great Western line between Castle Cary and Weymouth ran parallel for about a mile with the Yeovil Junction to Yeovil Town line from which this photograph was taken. The evening sun illuminates an unidentified GWR 'Grange' class 4-6-0 working a train from Weymouth, possibly the 17.50 departure which called at principal stations only. The train has just passed under the Southern main line under the bridge seen above the last coach of the train and will shortly pass by the connection between the two lines made in 1943 and known as Yeovil South Junction. This connection allowed through running between the GWR station to the east of the centre of Yeovil called Yeovil Pen Mill and Yeovil Junction. It was used for the shuttle service from Pen Mill after the closure of Yeovil Town in 1966 up to 1968 and has been retained for use as a diversionary route.

As noted previously, a regular shuttle service was maintained between Yeovil Junction and Yeovil Town station operated for many years by 'M7' class 0-4-4Ts and two coach sets known variously as rail motors or push-pull sets. With the Western Region takeover in 1963, GWR auto-fitted pannier tanks and Hawksworth trailer cars were introduced. Despite an attempt to replace them with '14xx' class 0-4-2Ts, the pannier tanks worked until replaced by diesel rail-buses in January 1965. Here an unidentified '64xx' class 0-6-0PT (possibly No 6435) propels its coaches towards Yeovil South Junction and Yeovil Junction station past Potter's Leaze Plantation with the two tracks of the Castle Cary to Weymouth line on the left.

ABOVE BR Class 5MT No 73080 swings round under Newton Road bridge with the Sundays only 09.35 local train to Exeter Central having just left Yeovil Town station on the other side of the bridge. The line on the right was a connection to the single line through Yeovil Town station that carried the Yeovil Pen Mill to Taunton services. Unusually at Yeovil Pen Mill and Yeovil Town, there was a single line with platform faces on both sides allowing boarding from the station buildings and interchange to the island platform. The Yeovil to Taunton passenger service was withdrawn on 7th July 1964, about a month before this picture was taken.

FACING PAGE TOP On a Sunday morning in July 1964, we look north from the slopes of Summer House Hill across the facilities at Yeovil Town. In the foreground on the right we see the yard and the western end of the Southern locomotive shed. Behind are the awnings and station building of Yeovil Town station and to the left the goods shed and part of the Great Western style signal box. Siding space appears to be at a premium on this day as the line alongside the goods shed normally used for loading vans has been pressed into service for passenger coaches.

All locomotive facilities had been concentrated at Yeovil Town shed since the closure of the Great Western shed at Yeovil Pen Mill in 1959, hence the presence of the GWR 0-6-0PT alongside 'West Country' class 4-6-2 *Blackmoor Vale* and 'U' class 2-6-0 No 31802.

FACING PAGE BOTTOM Excursion trains ran regularly on Sunday mornings from Exeter Central to Weymouth and, to avoid opening Yeovil South Junction signal box, the transfer from the Southern to the Great Western line was made via the Yeovil Town to Yeovil Pen Mill single line. In July 1964 the 10.15 Yeovil Town to Weymouth Sunday excursion has 'West Country' class 4-6-2 No 34100 *Appledore* and a miscellaneous collection of coaches including at least two Thompson LNER coaches on Gresley bogies. The locomotive will either run round to pull the coaches tender first to Yeovil Pen Mill or perhaps the steam near Newton Road bridge is a pilot locomotive. At Yeovil Pen Mill No 34100 will either run round or detach its pilot before proceeding past Yeovil South Junction on the Castle Cary to Weymouth line.

The above manoeuvres at Yeovil Pen Mill allowed ample time to drive the seven miles down the A37 from Yeovil to Holywell to take 'West Country' class No 34100 *Appledore* emerging from the Evershot Tunnel with the above train. The southern portal of the 308 yd long tunnel is the summit of a continuous climb of 5½ miles for down trains with the final two miles at 1 in 51/53. Hence the driver has the steam sanders on in case of slipping in the tunnel even with only a seven-coach train. The position of the Thompson coaches with the oval toilet windows confirms that the train has not reversed since seen at Yeovil Town.

On another occasion the same Sunday 10.15 Yeovil Town to Weymouth excursion was photographed approaching the northern portal of Evershot Tunnel hauled by 'West Country' class 4-6-2 34002 *Salisbury*. The rake contains Thompson vehicles as the first and third coaches and may be one of the sets of coaches that worked Summer Saturday services to and from the south coast and otherwise spent their time in sidings. Evershot station was just to the south of the Tunnel and its distant signal can be seen here alongside the permanent way hut. The catch point in the foreground to derail any wagons breaking away from a train was in the mind of any locomotive men whose train stalled in Evershot Tunnel. Most heavy trains would be banked from Yetminster to Evershot with the banker uncoupled from the train. If Evershot signal box was switched out, the banker would have to be coupled to the train and work through to Maiden Newton to cross over and return.

Back on the Southern main line, 'Battle of Britain' class 4-6-2 No 34086 *219 Squadron* is about to cross over the Great Western Weymouth line as it approaches Yeovil Junction with the 11.30 Brighton to Plymouth service in July 1964. No 34086 would have been attached to the train at Salisbury to return to its home shed Exmouth Junction, replacing a Brighton locomotive. There would be just under an hour for the Brighton locomotive to be serviced, turned and attached to the return Plymouth to Brighton train. The Yeovil Junction East or A signal box up advanced starter is seen on the left and was 349 yards from the signal cabin and placed on the top of the embankment to facilitate sighting on the right hand curve through the station and junction. The diamond on the signal indicates that the up line is track circuited here, thus saving footplate crew an awkward scramble to the telephone at the base of the signal. The signal wires in the down cess lead to the down home signals another 140 yards away.

The fireman of 'West Country' class 4-6-2 No 34003 *Plymouth* has the boiler under control as the crew await the right away with the 18.35 Yeovil Junction to Exmouth Junction freight in July 1964. The four grain-hopper wagons and empty milk tanks at the rear of the train are probably bound for Chard Junction being the first stop and the other traffics would be for successive stations. To the left of the train can be seen Yeovil Junction East or A signal box in the junction between the Yeovil Town lines to the left and the up main lines. In the distance between the signal box and the train can be seen the signal referred to in the previous picture. Its sighting on the top of the embankment makes it stand out clearly against the sky.

ABOVE Looking west to the Back Lane road bridge at Bradford Abbas east of Yeovil Junction, we see 'Battle of Britain' class 4-6-2 No 34059 *Sir Archibald Sinclair* on the Sundays only 11.48 local train from Yeovil Town to Salisbury. The horizontally bedded limestone that forms this higher land is strong enough to allow the sides of the lower cutting to be vertical however the softer upper strata have a shallow slope. Note that both up and down lines have been re-laid with flat bottom rails on concrete sleepers on the down line and wooden sleepers on the up line. However the 60 foot rail lengths are joined by fishplates rather than being welded to the delight of the train timers!

FACING PAGE TOP Although becoming a rarer sight in 1964, it was not uncommon, seen between Templecombe and Milborne Port, 'S15' class 4-6-0 No 30832 is making good time with the 11.10 all stations from Salisbury to Yeovil Town. The usual three-coach set has a full brake perhaps bound for the goods yard at Yeovil Town that handled a lot of parcels traffic. The 'S15' was a mixed traffic version of the 'King Arthur' class with smaller driving wheel diameter of 5ft 7in.

FACING PAGE BOTTOM 'Merchant Navy' class 4-6-2 No 35026 *Lamport & Holt Line* is in charge of the down 'Atlantic Coast Express' which is just breasting the summit at milepost 113½ near the village of Stowell. The train has just passed through Templecombe and the climb out of the valley of the River Cale includes a mile at 1 in 80 and nearly two miles at 1 in 100 but the descent from Buckhorn Weston Tunnel allowed this dip to be rushed. The fireman is clearly closing the firebox door between shovels as the patches of darker exhaust show.

A little further towards Templecombe from the previous picture, there is an attractive overbridge over the cutting. 'S15' class 4-6-0 No 30833 has no difficulty on the 1 in 100 descent with a three-coach local set on the Saturdays only 11.14 Salisbury to Yeovil Town stopping train. The concrete conduit covers in the cess on the up side reflect the conversion of the Templecombe up distant signal from a semaphore to the colour light signal just visible over the rear of the last visible coach of the 'Atlantic Coast Express' in the previous picture.

East of Templecombe the line dips down to the bridge over the River Cale before rising for 2½ miles at 1 in 90 to 100 through the 742 yards of Buckhorn Weston Tunnel to the summit at milepost 107½. 'Merchant Navy' class 4-6-2 No 35008 *Orient Line* on the Sundays only 12.20 from Exeter Central to Waterloo has not had to stop at Templecombe and so is able to use the momentum of the descent from Stowell to make good progress with its 11-coach train.

From the eastern portal of Buckhorn Weston Tunnel, the line continues to climb to the gradient post and then falls for a mile at 1 in 100 towards Gillingham. The driver of 'West Country' class 4-6-2 No 34002 *Salisbury* will have just closed the regulator to drift down to stop there with the 09.20 Exeter to Salisbury stopping train. There is an interesting contrast between the two vans at the head of the three-coach local set: the first van looks to be of LMS origin while the second van is the Southern Railway design.

Crossing to the north side of the line at the same location, 'Merchant Navy' class 4-6-2 No 35022 *Holland-America Line* has just passed under the Westbrook Road bridge to the east of Buckhorn Weston Tunnel with the down 'Atlantic Coast Express' (11.00 departure from Waterloo) in August 1964, the last complete month in which the train ran. Judging by the profiles of the first two coaches, this could be a scratch set possibly a relief to the main train.

ABOVE 'West Country' class 4-6-2 No 34107 *Blandford Forum* arrives at Semley with the 11.10 Salisbury to Exeter local train. The line here has climbed out of the valley of the River Nadder and now drops at 1 in 100 into the valley of the River Stour which it crosses at Gillingham. The road bridge at the west of the station carried the A350 Warminster to Shaftesbury road and in Southern Railway days the running-in boards were 'Semley for Shaftesbury'. Semley village proper is some 1½ miles to the east, the railway having generated its own community here. In addition to the goods facilities on the up side visible here, there was a healthy milk traffic to a siding to the west of the station. Noteworthy are the cattle vans at the cattle dock on the left, a reminder of a former important rail traffic now completely carried by road.

FACING PAGE TOP 'West Country' class 4-6-2 No 34019 *Bideford* is seen at West Hatch between Tisbury and Semley with a considerable down freight having to work hard up the 1 in 145 gradient. The first four vehicles could provide a 'fitted

head' to the train augmenting the brakes of the locomotive and rear brake van. As on many of the freight trains seen in this collection, containers on flat wagons were still widely used for small consignments. This traffic disappeared with the liberation of the tax regime for commercial vehicles in the 1960s that meant small vans were not restricted in their sphere of operation.

FACING PAGE BOTTOM 'Battle of Britain' class 4-6-2 No 34109 *Sir Trafford Leigh Mallory* has just passed Tisbury up home signal with the 16.00 Sundays only Waterloo to Exeter. The name is sometimes listed as 'Leigh-Mallory' but examination of photographs shows no hyphen on the nameplates. The fireman is building up the fire for the climb to Semley as the gradient steepens from 1 in 300 to 1 in 145. To the left of the up home signal can be seen the end of one of the distinctive round top awnings which were a feature of the up and down platforms at this station. The stationmaster's house and station buildings are hidden behind the trees.

An unidentified BR Class 4MT 2-6-0 approaches Tisbury with the daily milk empties that left Clapham Junction at about 16.00 for Exeter Central. The three leading tank wagons and coach came onto the train at Salisbury and the train spent over an hour at Templecombe detaching tanks for Bailey Gate via the Somerset and Dorset. Further tanks were detached at Chard Junction and Seaton Junction. The reason for the passenger coach is explained by the Working Timetable that notes that the train conveyed Second Class passengers only between Yeovil Junction and Chard Junction. However the coach attached on this day was one of the few Mark 1 Corridor Brake Composite (BCK) vehicles on the Southern Region. Possible explanations were delivery of a coach to Exeter after overhaul at Lancing or Eastleigh or forwarding of a coach that had been taken off another train for a mechanical problem, such as the brakes binding and requiring adjustment.

The line through Tisbury runs north east to south west so the light on a summer evening reflects off an up local train (16.42 Exeter to Salisbury) on the low embankment. 'West Country' class 4-6-2 No 34033 *Chard* will have no difficulty in keeping time with only three coaches as seven minutes were allowed for the five miles between Semley and Tisbury. The gradient is in favour of the locomotive so the engine will be working under very light steam.

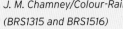

To end our journey following the route of the ACE we return to the far west – Padstow. The North Cornwall Railway opened to passenger traffic on 27 March 1899, and was to close on 1 January 1967. No 34033 *Chard* was a West Country stalwart being based at sheds in Devon and Cornwall for a number of years and is seen here in its last last month of action in the area in July 1964; reallocation to Eastleigh was to occur the following month. No 34033 is seen crossing the three span bridge over Little Petherick Creek, and then, a few minutes later, at the buffer stops.
J. M. Chamney/Colour-Rail (BRS1315 and BRS1516)